RECOGNITION OF REALITY

Reflections and Prose Poems

Adam Curle

HAWTHORN PRESS

Published by Hawthorn Press,
Bankfield House, 13 Wallbridge, Stroud, GL5 3JA, U.K.

First edition.

Typeset in Plantin by Glevum Graphics, 2 Honyatt Road, Gloucester.
Printed by A. Rowe, Chippenham, Wiltshire.
Cover photograph by Antony Moth, cover design by Patrick Roe.

Acknowledgements
Grateful acknowledgements are made to Bill & Nancy Frazer, Lanny Bradford Miller, Jane & Simon Fisher and Claire Toy for their help.

ISBN 1 869 890 12 4

Dedication

I dedicated my first book to my wife, Anne, thanking her among many other things, for preventing our baby, Deborah, from tearing up, eating or otherwise defacing the manuscript. Now Deborah is a wise, courageous and mature woman and I would like to dedicate this book to both her and Anne in great gratitude for very much happiness and for teaching me through their lives the best things I know about human nature.

I would also like to express my deepest thanks to Joanna Macy for what she is and what she does, and for writing the introduction to this book with her habitual generosity.

These pieces portray images, experiences and reflections recorded between June 1986 and June 1987.

Contents

Introduction

It is getting harder these days to escape the world and its pain. Each evening's news brings fresh reports of conflict and atrocities, of starvation and decimated rainforests and radioactive leaks. Each day's walk or drive can bring to our eyes, if we let ourselves see, the withering trees, the grim layers of smog, the homeless figures loitering in downtown doorways.

How do we deal with this? How do we respond to these evidences and portents of suffering? We can, of course, simply turn away. All of us do, to some extent; for there is much to distract us in our complicated comforts and ambitions. Or, our hearts flayed raw by accelerating dangers and injustices, we can respond with such desperation to do good that, run ragged between organizations and meetings and faced with frequent defeat of their causes, we burn out.

Or . . . there is a third alternative. We can so embrace the world that we move into it as into our own heart, compassionately recognizing its afflictions as extensions or mirror images of the conflicts and delusions we nurture in ourselves. When that movement – or stillness – of the mind occurs, something is released in us. Our firm grip on our separate selfhood dissolves and in its place springs a sense of identity with all life so real, so profound, that it can, buoying us like a river, be our strength and our hope.

I have met people who have shown me this is possible. Through grace or discipline they are able to detect through the world's pain a reality that sustains the actions they undertake for it. The Buddhist name for such beings is *bodhisattva*. There are, I believe, more of these humble heroes and heroines quietly at work in our world than we suspect. Yet few have been able to put down in words for us the searing and saving reality they have recognized.

Adam Curle would say – and does say in this extraordinary little volume of his – that his own words are "infinitely less" than the "truth (he) dimly senses." But I think they bring us about as close as we are likely to get to the inner reflections of a modern bodhisattva – and all the more persuasive for their remarkable lack of pretension. For what is offered us by this gentle, dogged servant of peace are not pieties about his or our innate nobility, but an honest, raw reporting of what he has seen and felt.

We need such disclosures now, for our own courage and sanity. For what Adam Curle lets us see through his eyes, and feel through his heart and mind, is both terrifying and triumphant.

We need to know that we can look straight into the face of a torturer, terrorist, or fraudulent official without averting our gaze. We need to know that we can see quite clearly the inhumanities they inflict and, at the same time, move through our own fear and loathing of them as through a curtain of fog. We need to know that the heart's ease and the spirit's joy are not to be found in flight from the suffering of our fellow-beings. They await us when we cease the search for a private salvation and when we escape the prison-cell of our personal righteousness.

Then, even in the these "last days," even "at this frayed end of the kalpa," "we gaze rapt at what survives, all things are wondrous . . . and we find beauty in each other."

Joanna Macy, October 1987.

Foreword

The writings that comprise this collection cluster, in general, around three themes:

The habits of thought, especially our understanding of and attitude towards ourselves and others (essentially a spiritual distortion but also one embodied in and expressed through many of our social institutions) that lead to the great perils and miseries of the planet and its people – war, poverty, oppression, fear-filled hatred of strangeness, and the desecration and destruction of the environment.

Particular examples of perils and miseries to which these ways of thinking have led. The situations and incidents described are all ones in which I have been directly or indirectly involved, largely through work over many years on Third World poverty and conflict; readers can no doubt multiply them from their own experience. In most cases I have not identified the events described, though some will certainly recognise some of them as relating to the Indian Sub-Continent, West Africa (especially the Nigerian civil war), Southern Africa in general, or Northern Ireland as well as being caricatures of the behaviour of Western nations. There are two reasons for this reticence. Firstly, such details might embarrass those trying to help; secondly, I don't want to give the impression that such happenings are confined to specific times and places; they are, alas, mere symptoms of a global sickness that we should understand as such. Nevertheless, they do not constitute the reality referred to in the title. They are aspects of a second order of reality, one the Tibetans refer to as deceptive, conditional or relative. They do not arise from truth, but from illusions and distorted perceptions which they perpetuate by masking awareness with fear, craving, hatred and ignorance.

The third theme, by contrast, is the spiritual, the *ultimate reality* – another Tibetan term – which is our fundamental being. This, to the extent that we *recognise* it (in the sense of remembering and understanding *again* what we have in our deeper parts always known), will weaken the forces of despairing extermination and the states of mind and society that spawn them. Complete recognition will eliminate them completely.

These poems and reflections are not arranged here in terms of theme. As in life, they are interwoven and the motifs often overlap.

Adam Curle, Summer, 1987.

1
The First Lesson

The most important lesson
but one that's seldom adequately learned
is that, like sub-atomic particles,
everything with life exists
within a field of force
in which all affect and are affected
by each one of the others;
and that we, the individuals,
and all other individuals like
a blade of grass, whale or bacterium,
are not self-existent, but the products
of this unceasing reciprocity.

When this interaction favours
growth and fruitful change
we call it ecologically sound,
understanding that death and demolition
are part of the process
of development –
Kali is goddess both of creation and destruction.

But when this interaction
is impaired by false beliefs,
illusions one might say, of personal
supremacies and needs,
elements within the field of force
may be eliminated
or suffer deadly damage.

Through war, poverty imposed
by others' greed, oppressive persecution
and gluttonous violations of the planet
whole tribes, forests, civilisations, fish-filled seas,
species, forms of art, religions
are annihilated.

The total field is then impoverished
and many lives
one might have thought quite separate
are dismally affected;
our choices are diminished,
the scope of evolution narrows down.

We best can counter this
by widening our vision of the truth
and acting in accordance with it.

2
Optimism

My poems are pessimistic, says my wife.
In one sense she's absolutely right –
Humanity has got its knickers
Into the most ineluctable twist;
The effect of our follies, evil, ignorance,
Everything that Buddhists call unskilful means,
Is cataclysmic
Crying out to be recorded and condemned.

But I don't think we are now worse,
Greedier or more selfish,
Only that the means of destruction
And of organising rapacity
Have been improved and institutionalised
By means unknown to our forebears.

Of course I wish things were different –
No nuclear weapons, pollution, venal
Politicians, cash-crazed businessmen,
Cruel and corrupt regimes,
Etcetera.
But however dangerous and painful
Are these things, they rate extremely low
On the scale of reality.
They are illusions that the human mind
Projects upon the screen of consciousness.
They may starve, torture, poison,
Or disintegrate our bodies,
But these too are illusions.

The truth is utterly other. It's in
The finer forms of energy we sense
Through loving and awareness of great beauty,
In sudden glimpses shown us of
The void, formless yet the source of all form,
The indestructible kingdom of heaven
Within and without (whatever these
Terms, in themselves meaningless, suggest).
This truth is with us always,
Eternal well of wonder and delight,
Of compassion and wisdom,
If we awake to the beginningless
And never ending present,
Free of nostalgia or sorrow for the past
And terror or expectation for the future.
Then, knowing that reality
Is both lovely and invulnerable,
We dare feel hope.

3
The Solicitous Terrorist

'I don't think it's quite wise' said the guerrilla,
Solicitous for my well-being,
'To stay in that hotel,
It could be on our hit list'.
(You might call him a terrorist
But he suffered first and hasn't
Inflicted more than he endured.
This isn't meant as an excuse;
Rather, an explanation.)

Nor is it wise to fly on this plane or that,
It might be hijacked or blown up
(The long downward hurtle after an explosion
Is my pet phobia.)
But neither is it wise to be a Black in South Africa,
A peasant in Central America,
A Palestinian on the West Bank,
A pygmy in Zaire,
A Chakma in Bangladesh
Or one of far too many other groups to name –
Not that you've much choice.

Placed as you are
You rebel against the suffering
Of your people, or put up with it.
Either way, you and your children die,
Usually too young.
Either way the comfortable hate you
And exorcise their fear with shuddering names
Like terrorist.

Yet my terrorist,
With no well-being of his own to care for,
Yet worried about mine
Took my hand in his two bloodied ones.

4
The Policeman Calls

We wait for it knowing it must come
– but when? – the dreaded visitation;
at length, while we sleep uneasy,
there it is, the midnight call,
that quintessential happening of our age;
I dress slowly, fumbling, trying to gain time
to put my wits together.
The darkness standing by my bed:
'get a move on, you, he's waiting'.

He, the secret policeman, gross with authority,
a mauling beast with male suspects,
capable of strangling an obstinate
prisoner in the cells bare handed,
yet somehow shifty, ill at ease with women;
thinning sandy hair, lumpy face,
spreading buttocks that overflow the chair,
blank saurian stare, bludgeoning first words:
'we know how to make you talk, professor'.

Must I give in to fear and loathing
eventually living in the mire
of having squealed out confessions
that implicate my friends;
or manage to retain awareness that
behind the ugly mask of illusion
hides the reality, the potential for enlightenment,
the ground of all being
from which emerge, only to return
and mingle inextricably,
policeman, professor, prisoner
and the intimidating women.
If so I may be stronger to resist.

5

Recognition of Reality

At times my weary old perceptions,
over exposed to dreadful happenings,
see only the very worst realities:
war with its reek of blood and bodies,
crunch of bone splatting shells,
fear that sweats away your soul;
the fat landlord's tyranny
spurring hopeless rebellion
and gruesome retribution;
poverty, the gnawed faces
of disease, pathetic twig limbs
and balloon guts of hunger.
They seem so deadly real.

But behind these facts,
another level of reality:
nothing is separate, all together weave
an endless web of shifting
interplay, an ever changing
but harmonious tapestry.

But when we recognise it not, lack
transcendent vision, seeing only
the separate and contending
fates of every being, we live
an illusion; we yearn, envy,
struggle with those who are ourselves,
ghost shadows boxing in a hall of mirrors.

Remember too that recognition means
To know again, to recall
what was always known but forgotten,
part of our human heritage
of sacred wisdom.

6
Enemies

Implacably hostile factions brought together
Through Joe's brilliant diplomatic sleight
In a remote mountain village
To discuss interests they had in common
Perhaps transcending political differences –
Jobs, homes, public services, above all
A decent future for their kids.

At first things really didn't look too good;
Suspicious dogs circling each other, legs stiff, necks
Abristle, ears back, ominous low snarls.
Lucky they'd had to leave their guns behind
And the Prods been guaranteed safe conducts.

They'd never met, but knew each other well
By reputation. Myths of cruelty
And violence cloaked the fighters, making
Them archetypal figures of
Terror and destruction.

But contiguity worked magic,
Supplemented by Guinness and Bushmills
Irish whisky mellowing into song.
Soon, if only for a day,
They know each other as they really were,
Human beings, Irishmen, fellow unfortunates and heroes,
Friends.

Even if, later, they only saw each other
Through the sights of an armalite rifle
Perhaps this glimpse of true oneness would not
Leave them entirely unchanged.

7
Liberation

How liberating – oh the light and lightness –
to discard the false identity,
to discover that the importunate I
we so desperately cherished,
nearly killing servile bodies
in the process, so heavy is the strain
of incessant fabrication,
is nothing, an illusion.
It exists nowhere in the swirl
of shifting thoughts memories and feelings
(fine playground for the psychotherapists)
which flicker constantly across
the mental radar screen.
No need to worry about keeping up
appearances or about what they
(those other illusions we call Bill or Mary)
think of us, especially what
we think about ourselves
for there is, wonderful discovery,
no self to think about;
released from this burden we know freedom.

Bill and Mary don't yet understand;
now what's all this, they ask,
about the non-reality of self;
of course it's real, it's *you*; what else could be?

What else indeed. The proper nature,
once stubborn I has melted,
both hears and plays the music of the void;
is the light of eternity
and the prism that refracts it;
is one with all things yet unique;
loves all beings without distinction
or need for return;
this is life abundant.

It always was, in truth,
except that we in ignorance
constructed cages for our dwellings
and shadows to inhabit them.

8
The Deluded Unrighteous

We refer to the deluded
As unrighteous and indeed they act
unpleasantly, but it's not for us
To judge them, only to define
The pattern of their dominant illusions.

The most deluded of this age are not just
straightforward crooks swindlers embezzlers
twisters cheats and shady dealers. That too,
perhaps, but many of them also hold
high office, are respected in the city,
well known in smart society, seen at
Henley and Ascot and the centre court
at Wimbledon; and all the American
equivalents. Some are believing
Christians (many being born-againers).
Even if not particularly pious
they are selfrighteously assured
of moral worth, smugly intolerant of
heretics and dissidents of every sort
social sexual sartorial or even
doctrinal. Projecting outward what Jung
calls the shadow, they turn them into fiends
on whom they gladly sick their MI5,
their Contras, Special Branch or CIA.
They often lecture the unfortunate
victims of their callous policies
and dogma that the rich are better than
the poor, berating them for fecklessness
and lack of the Victorian virtues,
(which they of course have done too well to need)
thriftiness, honesty, sobriety.
It's wasteful, they complain among themselves,
to educate these yobbos any more
than needed to perform their brainless tasks

or keep them living past their working prime.
Good people push ahead, join BUPA, send
their kids to decent schools, buy all they want.
God who helps those who help themselves, they say,
sensibly worked the whole thing out that way.

9
Who Am I?

Well, I am not to be confused with a particular body, the jobs
it has carried out, its role in society, its appearance and
behaviour good bad or indifferent, least of all the ego it thinks
of as 'I' and the opinions that nourish it however wise or silly.

Oh, no denying there is a grouping of attributes faculties
tendencies awarenesses and elements apparently possessing, though
forever changing their balance and their place, the random quirks and
qualities known as Adam Curle.

But who can say it's 'I'?

Let's take another look. The particles momentarily coalesced in this
being streamed from gassy stars and grew in primeval sludge at
various epochs over a beginningless time, fused and separated again in
myriad forms of life, constituted the focus for countless
consciousnesses of which a minute fraction may have attained a
measure of wisdom and compassion.

In slime in water in the air in earth as creatures or corpuscles
viruses enzymes chemicals grasses cows codfish cockroaches humans
they played their part.

Each concatenation thought itself an 'I', made myths; even whole
civilisations were woven around this 'I', this false identity.

But the proper function of this fusion
is to form a dwelling for the real identity,
the potential for enlightenment.

10
Lament for a Tribe

The people, a simple yet sophisticated
Buddhist tribe, artistic and peaceful,
protected by paternalistic Brits,
stood very little chance against
their own government,
whose first unfeeling crime
against the people and their land
was to erect a monstrous dam.
'A few tribals may be flooded out',
officials mentioned casually,
'when the waters have backed up.
Compensation? Oh yes, I suppose so'.

The water came, filling the fertile valleys
of the tribal villages.
No proper place to go;
the hills steep, densely forested,
useless for cultivation;
so called settlement areas
shack-slums washed out
by the monsoon.
The hundred thousand tribals
(not the official 'few')
ceased to be a people.
Without the village net-work
all social bonds were weakened.
Men drifted to the coastal towns
they always had avoided,
became tubercular and syphilitic.

'Too bad,' officials said, 'but these chaps
are really good-for-nothings.
They simply squander handouts
instead of getting down to work
and making a new start.'

Then, cheerfully, 'but only think
of all the benefits the dam will bring
to the whole nation. Power
for industry, irrigation,
better scope for inland waterways'.
But they'd botched it.
Someone had forgotten that
lake water levels rise much quicker
when rain falls directly on the surface
than when it trickles down
a million mountain runnels.
This, added to some serious structural flaws,
nearly destroyed the dam, silted
up the waterways, burst the banks
of irrigation channels,
so no one profited at all
(except of course consultants
and contractors from abroad
who'd pocketed their fees and pushed off
long ago).

But the harm was done.
Their best land taken by the worthless waters,
their homes submerged,
their young men gone,
the tribe was deadly stricken.

Then, while the dam was gradually
restored to some poor semblance
of efficiency,
the government began to turn
an envious eye upon the
surviving tribal territory.
'They're only Buddhists, after all,
illiterate primitives and incompetent farmers'.

It took not much to turn
already smouldering resentment
into enraged defiance,
thus providing plausible excuses

to raid the settlements,
corral the men in labour camps,
molest the women, massacre the monks
in the name of suppressing terrorism,
a sacred cow-like phrase which,
as does 'national security',
gilds the cruel and ridiculous
with patriotic tinsel.

Now many of the tribal people
flee across the borders,
their poor harvests abandoned,
hamlets deserted save for the
half-life of the very old.
A few lurk desperate in the hills,
armed with ancient guns,
feuding among themselves
(ironically a frequent
outcome of oppression)
and occasionally issue out
to kill a sentry or blow up a bridge,
thus bringing fearful retribution
on anyone the soldiers find to slaughter.
(Which naturally facilitates
land appropriation through
the sponsored scheme of settlement
for suitable non-tribal 'cultivators'.)

I saw the beginning of this tragedy,
alas no freak phenomenon,
some thirty years ago, did what I could
– how little – to avert it.
Now I am a mourner at the funeral.

11
The Girl

Coming from the pharmacist
With the medicine I'd been told to take
For a minor ear infection
Before flying (the pressure might affect it)
I saw a young girl's figure silhouetted
In the doorway, hand outstretched for alms,
Bright sun behind her making the
Face invisible.
As I approached I realised there was
Another reason why I couldn't see it;
She didn't have one,
Only bones, teeth, gristle, the stump of a nose,
Eyes, eyes.
Ashamed and horrified I gave her
All I had, but of course nothing could restore
The sloughed off flesh
(A not unusual consequence, I'm told
Of typhoid or prolonged dysentery).

Clutching my self-indulgent medicine
I fled, symbol of the rich unfeeling west;
Behind me, the girl still stands,
Irreparably harmed, indirect
Victim of the affluent ethos
That made me so concerned
About my petty pains,
So able to assuage them.

12
The Last Days

Just see where it's got us,
Our desperate try to compensate
For feeling unlovable, bereft or bad
Having almost lost awareness
Of the Self.

The only measure left, to build
A false identity that's based
On meaningless material achievement
Making us for a trivial span
Feel good.
Stricken forests, lethal lakes,
Pasture turned to desert,
Razed hedges, filled in ponds,
Lost species, slaughtered tribes,
The price we pay for briefly boosted
Sense of worth.

At this frayed end of the kalpa*
How hungry are our people,
How desperate the rich. They too
Are suffering from famine –
Of the spirit.
The products of our violated world,
Nuclear arsenals and other
Technological trinkets,
Gratify no longer. What's left
But self-destruction?

Those conscious of the swift unravelling
Gaze rapt at what survives,
All things are wondrous,
A speedwell, a moving ant,
The flight of any undistinguished bird,
An old woman or a baby.

We who are left become one,
Honour and find beauty in each other,
Recognise the common ground of life
While it yet endures.

* In Hindu cosmology one of the great ages of the world. We live in the last, the so-called Iron Kalpa.

13
Religious Rivals

The Deacon and his rival,
Another pastor of souls,
Supposedly his ally,
Both kept private armies.
These did a first class job of
Disciplining villagers
Thought to be recalcitrant,
Burning their homes, raping their
Wives, chopping them up
With pangas.* But the Deacon,
In the holy name of national
Defence, decided that the other
Gang had got a bit too strong,
So he made the rival reverend
A very tempting offer:

Get all your men together in such
And such a place;
I'll issue them
With smart new uniforms.

Having only rather scruffy gear,
They assembled merrily.
The crafty Deacon then sent in
The helicopter gunships
And wiped out most of them;
Surviving wounded were disposed of
In a mineshaft.

To meet the Deacon you might not
Think butter would melt in his
Mouth; reasonable, friendly,
Not too bright, popular with the Brits
(Who don't like smart-assed natives).
Funny that his Christian name
Was Abel. It should have been
The other brother.

* Long, broad-bladed slashers.

14
Indra's Net

At each intersection of the endless net
of Indra's heaven, according to the myth,
is a bead that represents a human life.
Each bead reflects every other
and every reflection of every other.

In the sub-atomic field each hadron
affects and is affected by all the rest,
resulting in a flux of energy and movement
in which little can be foretold
save unpredictability and endless change.

The boundaries between us are hallucinations,
we are indeed members of one another,
dancing together spontaneously like the hadrons,
containing each other like the beads.

15
Roots of Violence

James, in his epistle, considering why
we war and quarrel with each other,
says it's because of lust or craving
for things we haven't got and can't get
otherwise; we're envious and hence
dissatisfied, and if we ask, we ask
amiss, so no one answers.

Buddhists blame yearning and attachment
which broadly means we focus the libido
on things that cannot gratify for long,
a situation that we try correcting
by means that only bring more pain
and in the end may lead to violence.

The military pundits will object
this is too simple to explain the great
upheavals that from time to time engulf
the world. Possibly. But the ways of thought
necessitating armies, patriotic pride,
territorial ambitions and the like
originated in the myth that
what we have and do will really solve
the problems of ourselves.

16
Quakers

Of all the groups I know, the Quakers,
With whom I unworthily associate,
Can most be relied on for wise
Compassion, common sense and
Serious commitment to issues
Affecting spiritual
And physical well being
Of virtually anyone anywhere
In the world.
                    Oh, yes, I know they
Sometimes get things wrong, or seem
A bit conventional, but always,
In the end, they turn up trumps
As I well know experimentally
(George Fox's phrase).
                              They don't care much
For dogmas, but believe in
The essential divine goodness of
Our being, exploring its deeps
Together in their worship,
Then surfacing refreshed, illuminated
By the Inner Light, strengthened
For the work they see ahead.

17
The Spoils of War

The young commander, exhausted and exultant,
sprawled on his seat reporting his apparent
victory; the enormous convoy
trapped on the long causeway, no escape,
exploded ammo trucks blocking front and rear
with sodden jungle lapping either side,
was suffering slow piecemeal destruction.

He thought, in his tired high, he'd won the war.
Ah, but he hadn't, no one ever does.
The so-called victors will become aware,
though trying to ignore the evidence,
their fight for justice or for liberation
(let alone a less high-sounding cause)
by some grim logic spawns the opposite;
prison walls darken the land, the vultures
flop gorged around the slaughter houses,
at dawn the secret police still make their calls,
the myriad mourners are uncomforted,
there's something precious everyone has lost.

How many men and how much hope must die
to turn a triumph into a defeat
making all talk of victory a lie?

18
Black Flies

I admit to prejudice against black flies,
They are too keen on things I also like –
Nasturtiums, tansy and broad beans,
But it's unreasonable to blame them
For sharing my tastes, it only shows
They are discriminating sentient beings!

Not long ago we pulled up several
Badly infested nasturtium plants
And left them for disposal near the door.
Next day I studied them. The black flies
Were all dead,
The underside of umbrella leaves
A scene of catastrophic carnage.
The creatures, while alive my enemies,
Lay in distorted postures there amid
The detritus of their existence.
No movement. Nothing. Each one done for.

And here am I, a person who purports
To work for peace among humans,
Pressing the nuclear button, as it were,
Without a moment's thought.
What right have I to hope for better treatment?

19
The Rule of Evil

Under the rule of evil
Love everywhere turns cold
When air is rank with selfish greed
The youngest hearts feel old
And now we're all infected
Our rulers have done well
To teach that all we need to do
Is learn to buy and sell
That profit is the road to heaven
(Did some fool mutter 'hell'?)

The first two lines are taken, more or less word for word, from what I recently saw written on a young man's T shirt.

20
The Raid on the Terrorist Camp

The government announced they had
Successfully attacked and
Eliminated a terrorist
Stronghold. They had first bombed
And strafed a group of huts and houses
Some distance from the town.
Then squads of special forces had been
Landed from two large helicopters.
They rushed the shattered buildings
Blazing away and hurling grenades
To wipe out the survivors –
Three old men, two women and several
Small children. Already dead
Were more women and babies, too fragmented
For accurate body count, and some goats.
This only proves that communist
Subversion recognises no
Barriers of age or sex.

After locating a cache of
Important secret documents disguised as
Primary school readers and a
Manual on water conservation
(Cunning bastards, these commies)
They blew up
The last remaining hut, then very
Pleased with this efficient operation,
Withdrew in good order,
Signalling to headquarters:
Mission successfully accomplished.

21

Mediation/Meditation

An easy mistake, I often
Type meditation for mediation
And vice versa,
Slightly amused at the difference
The letter T makes to the meaning.

But perhaps it's not so great;
In meditation we become
More aware of reality,
Escaping from automatism
Of habitual responses
And from enslavement to
Our negative emotions.
Thus freed we live and love with
Greater strength and greater understanding
And so, among other things,
Can mediate with more effect.

We hope through mediation
To purify the atmosphere
Of needless (some's inevitable)
Suspicion, angry fear and
Misconception that impede accord.
We try in fact to introduce
Reality into the furious
Fantasies swathing both
Protagonists who now see each
Other not as human but demonic.
In this uneasy kinship
That we have with two hostile groups
We strive, as in our meditation,
To bring awareness.

But it is hard.
We only gain the measure of success
Achieved within ourselves –
Not always even that.

22
Cyanide

The guerrillas always carry with them
Cyanide capsules in case of capture.
If too badly wounded for escape
They ask their friends to shoot them in the head
Or else take the poison.
                                        It doesn't
Always work at once and some soldiers,
Knowing this, try to make their last moments
As agonising as possible. One
Was tied behind a jeep and dragged along
A stony road, shoulders dislocated.
Others had cigarettes stubbed out on their
Eyeballs. (An ingenious procedure
With prisoners whom there's time to torture
Slowly, is pushing live serpents down
Their throats.) Small wonder the guerrillas do
Their best not to be taken alive.

One day, far from the battle lines, I took
An evening stroll, tripped, fell and cut my face.
At once I was surrounded by charming
And solicitous young people, concern
Etched on pleasant faces, wanting to help;
The brothers and sisters of those
Torturers.

23
Concessions?

Why not, I urged, try some small concession,
A local cease fire perhaps,
To break the deadlock.
A slight reduction in the level
Of violence sometimes makes
An atmosphere more favourable to
Reasonable negotiation instead of
Reciprocal mudslinging.

The general, brooding glumly over maps,
Wrenched his attention from the last report
(A disastrous one),
But answered patiently
'You don't know these people,
Animals,' he said, 'savages;
Only understand the language of the gun,
Respect you for using it.
Oh yes, I know their tricks,
Been fighting them for years'.
Turning heavily to the maps once more,
Adds over his shoulder
'Can't afford to take risks,
Got to keep the pressure on,
Let up a second and they take the chance
To regroup or claw at us again'.

General, you've often said
No one can win this sort of war.
You've got to talk to each other
Some time; why not now?
It might just work, I think.
Admitted there's a danger
They'll take advantage of a lull,
But they say just the same of you.
Someone's got to start the process

And surely you can guard against
Most breaches of the truce,
But not to take a chance for peace
Is to ensure, no gamble here,
Continued bloodshed.

He considers; grunts 'Possibly,
But you realise I'll have to
Discuss it with the cabinet'.

Does he agree; is this a cautious
Hint of shifting policy,
Or just a way of getting rid
Of me without further argument?
I go away wondering about
The whole crazy business:
What gives us the mandate
To decide officially to kill each other;
To conscript armies, order attacks,
Feeling complete justification
(Perhaps tinged with regret,
But probably not).
How many men will die, I speculate,
Before I meet the general again.

24
Waiting at the Airport

Endlessly waiting at the airport
While storms clear, engines are repaired
Or, often, for no revealed reason.
The indefinite delay seems intolerable.
The so-called restaurant/snack bar is shut,
When it opens there will be
A few buns, genuine local antiques
Much appreciated by flies
And several bottles of tepid Limca.
The seats very hard, set at awkward angles,
Flaccid air clings like a warm damp cloth.
No chance of getting out to wander
Around once we are processed through
(A tedious business anyway);
The police with suspicious rifles
Wave us crossly back.

At first we are peevish, fume impotently –
How can we bear to stew and starve
So bored, so uncomfortable,
But all at once, surprisingly,
We find ourselves accepting it.
Instead of tedium, delightful free hours,
No trespassing telephone, no sudden
Domestic crisis to interfere
With enjoyment of thought, meditation
Or writing poetry (always take a pen).
Incomprehensible announcements for
Other passengers flow over us unheeded –
We don't care that other flights are
Now departing, delayed or cancelled.

With benign detachment we observe
Fretful passengers with whining children,
Handbaggage festooned around them
(Who said one piece only?)
Plastic bags, buckets containing
Mysterious foodstuffs wrapped in leaves,
Sacking elaborately sewn up
That customs will at once demand undone,
People hopeful, sad, confused, resigned.

We long term waiters have been
Insulated from the noise and chaos
Like water spiders in their globe of air
Safe from the surrounding flood.

Suddenly a wonderful event;
The torpid snack bar jerks to life.
Eager men, hasting from the depths,
Bring platters of spiced rice,
Trays of bowls containing chicken soup,
Vegetable and fish curry, pickles,
A super lunch for only 40p.
At once crowds of airport staff
Joking and jolly,
Gobbling up the food or taking
Packed cardboard boxes
To lairs in customs shed, flight control,
Security, accounts, maintenance;
Gladly we join the queue.

Eventually the flight is called;
We half regret emerging to the world of time.
The immigration line, we note,
Has barely moved a yard in
Seven minutes, customs slower still,
Checking-in seems endless.
At last, anticlimactically, we board the plane.

Now ordinary life resumes.
Nuclear submarines prowl
Beneath the ice floes,
The rockets in their subterranean silos
Point mindless annihilation
At humanity misled
By false beliefs and crazy leaders.
While we waited the suffering earth
Could have been destroyed
Ten times over.

The steward brings a trolley round with drinks,
We order eagerly.

25
The Antique President

The antique president quite cleverly
Managed to say two contradictory
Things in the same interview:
There would be no negotiations
Until the terrorists were all wiped out;
And he would be happy to negotiate
With any one at any time.
So is he gaga, or so cunning that
He doesn't mind appearing to seem gaga?
If the latter,
Just whom is he trying to confuse and why?

The guerillas, but there's little point in
That because anyway they always draw
The worst conclusions from everything
He says.

The members of the cabinet,
In order to set them against each other
Instead of banding together
To oust him.

The political opposition,
So that they won't know on which ground
To oppose him.

The numerous social and religious
Factions with mutually exclusive
Aspirations, so that there'll be something
To please them all,
Making him popular with everyone.

To influence the aid consortium, the IMF
And the World Bank, who will hear
What suits them.

To make everyone, allies and enemies alike,
Wonder about Alzheimers disease
And whether the old boy's senile and
If so what the hell to do
About it,
Thus creating an atmosphere of
Uncertainty that leaves him free
To do precisely what he wants.

So what might that be?

Well, in a long and sadly not yet
Extinguished political career
He has consistently served two
Reciprocal ideals:
The humiliation and exclusion
Of a particular minority group he dislikes;
And the preservation and enhancement
Of his own power.
If the tactics of the moment have
Demanded an occasional softening
Of either principle,
The long term strategy has never deviated.

But if eventually it's clear to all
That he's gone right round the bend,
What next?

There'll probably be a pretty bloody
Free for all, and may the best man
(Or probably in this case, woman)
Win.
Or the party now in power, much
Though all the members loathe each other,
Will stay in office using him
As figure head, eventually
Stuffing the old reptile,
Automating him, filling his
Electronic brain with pre-recorded
Speeches like a monster from
Science fiction.

Which, in fact, he already is.

26
Hope and the Prisoner

Hope, a most beguiling golden ball
Tossed within reach which, if I catch it,
Turns to dirty yellow.

'Just tell us what you've learned about these
People. They're not your sort, you know; they're
Proper shits to let you carry the can.
You owe it to yourself to tell the truth.
Now we don't want to get nasty with you
But one way or the other we'll find out,
You bet we will. So why not save yourself
The trouble. Come clean and we'll let you go
At once. No charges, nothing.
But just remember, no soft business here
Of being innocent until proved guilty.
As far as I'm concerned, you're guilty now,
We can keep you here indefinitely
And when you are sentenced it will be for
Ten years at least, plotting against the state's
A very serious crime, it could be
Death in fact. So let's start. Now then,
Who are the men referred to in this letter?
(He reads a passage) No? Well, I believe
These men are terrorists. Don't try to
Protect them. If they are innocent they
Won't be harmed; if not, you should be as glad
As me to see them behind bars where they
Belong. (He sits back) It's up to you
To choose the hard way or the easy.'

He juggles with the ball of hope. Perhaps
Some trivial facts would satisfy him?
But no, once I began to give there'd be
No end, the beans would all be spilt.
Drop dead, deceitful hope. Let me concentrate
On confusing and outwitting them.

27
The Lama

He teaches us by simply being.
His presence, *Kündün,*
Opens a third eye
To see the other world, the true one,
Not one we've fabricated
Of illusion.
Now in his light we know again
What we had forgotten,
Miracles, gifts of poetry
Or music, things that family,
School or convention, the so-called
'Real world', blotted from awareness.

He gives us no new knowledge,
The truth is already with us;
Trendy fresh ideas and notions
Are ephemeral – instead
He shows us how to exercise
Psychic muscles for unblocking
The mind's channels, to release
Arcane wisdom within the heart,
To join the woman and the man
In our own being.

The teachings do not aim to rouse
Peculiar abilities –
Levitation, clairvoyance,
The bag of tricks called *siddhis*,
But to naught the blustering ego
Whose demands destroy compassion;
Then only can we really
Fulfil our proper task, helping
Others reach enlightenment.

28
Africa

It's sickening to think how much
We, the slavers, thieving settlers, exploiters and such
Like muck have messed the whole place up,
Canting, culture-killing missionaries, corrupt
Traders in arms, junk, worthless drugs,
Smart alec experts, skads of smug
Officials, clowns all certain that they knew
What's best for 'natives'. This sorry crew
Have bled, starved, robbed, attacked,
Belittled, divided, racked,
Incestuously raped this mother land
The womb from which came all of humankind.

Allow me a pause to calm an angry mind
Before I pay humble tribute to the men
And women, so patient, so forgiving. When
I would have long since yielded to hating,
They obstinately forbore, awaiting
A change of heart that never came,
Only more cunning hidden pillage; aid now the name
For modern theft, but the result the same.

But not many really understand
Our implication in the sorrow of that land.
Once when I told a friendly man that we
Had lived some years in Africa, he
Answered 'Africa, eh?' Reflected, then said
'A lot of trouble with the niggers there, I've read'.

29
Human Reponsibility

We human beings hold the world's resources
in trust for each other,
but a majority of the trustees
have embezzled what should
be shared with all the rest.
And sadly the majority
fail to recognise that other beings
have any rights at all.
We enslave and exploit these creatures,
poison and destroy their habitats,
but if they want revenge
(and I suspect they're far too kind for that)
they'll get it:
what we've done to them and to each other
will also do us in.

30

Co-operating Enemies

The first is a fossil lizard,
diplodocus ancient,
glow-worming a glint of life.
Frustrated for a couple of decades
by rich and haughty families
he'd no real power until seventy
but now he clings on crazily
and means to die in office.
Peace in the loathsome war could be
disastrous to this aim,
ending the emergency would cause
an election he might lose.
So, while scoring points for seeming
bent upon a reasonable
settlement, but not losing them by
appearing weakly eager, he
cleverly frustrates patient Eirene
just when she seems to have it made;
a document is shredded or disappears,
a sponsored leak occurs,
a mediator is accused of bungling
or partiality and in the flurry
peace vanishes again.
Then all the cabinet who, like their boss,
are profiteers of war,
gleefully contrive a few more scenes
to act in the charade.

His adversary,
though fifty years the younger,
would also sooner die than lose
the power now dearer than his blood.
No compromise for him,
no second best, no give and take,
no pity for his suffering people
Still hunted and tormented.
No way; the more the merrier.
Each added horror fuels
more furious resistance
– and so, of course, no peace.

Odd how these two men collaborate
to play each other's game.

31
Preserving the Nuclear Peace

There is a far too widely held
belief in the delusion
that preserving peace
depends upon the weaponry,
conventional and nuclear,
to maintain a proper balance,
one that deters attack
by either side.

Agreed that it's precarious,
that every advance in
nuclear technology
may rock an already shaky
equilibrium,
thus driving the other side to costly
investment in research
and arms development –
and so on and spiralling on.
But this just illustrates,
our leaders dogmatise,
the price we have to pay
for nuclear peace.

Somewhere along the line
our vision narrows. We don't see
our enemies as human
but embodied evil,
full of hatred, violence and greed,
slavering to destroy us,
held back by fear alone:
the mirror image of how *they* see *us*.
Sharing this sick perception,
we both are terrified and seek for solace
in our arsenals.

Thus we empower *things*
and have consigned our fate
to metal and explosive
as if they had superceded
human wisdom and understanding,
and were able of themselves
to decide on peace or war.

How to revoke this abject
abrogation of what makes us
men and women?
Simply to realise what
we are doing to ourselves,
halving our humanity,
should jolt us into shame,
make us recollect that we
and those we've made our enemies
are not mere puppets on the strings of fear,
slaves of the missile,
but conscious beings
having hopes and needs and loves
that are identical.

Recalling that, it must be possible
to keep the peace by using
mind and heart.

32
Professors

George Fox had trouble with professors
And so, being also one, do I,
Especially with myself.

Though mine are the sort in cap and gown
While his professed a dogma,
Some heavy piece of God-stuff,
Both lots are much the same.

They brim with notions and opinions,
On which they hang a sense of self,
Struggling to preserve it from
Heretical dissent. Their swollen
Heads aswirl with prideful fury
They drain all love and foolishness from
Shapeless bodies dwarfed by logic.

The poor professors haven't understood
How too much head-work dissipates the good
Whose source within our being
Is the heart sensing and the eye seeing.

33
Mind

Long years ago I saw, the inner
eye still sees, a small round pond
in the midst of a far off forest,
the water limpid but so deep
the eye could reach no bottom.
Once while I gazed a monstrous fish,
first a dim shadow far below
but then increasingly magnificent,
rose to the surface, made itself known
then slowly sank from sight to where
I felt certain that this single pool
must join with countless others in an
immeasurable subterranean lake.

But fallen leaves would often cover
much of the pond's surface.
I might have described it then
by the intricate pattern,
always different and shifting,
that they made, as one might say,
conventionally trivial,
someone has this quality or that,
pleasant or not according to
capricious taste, oblivious of clear
profundities below and magical
beings that inhabit them,
gliding mysterious wise and calm
throughout the hidden lake of mind.

34
Our Hive

Our hive seethes with purposefully
aberrant life, all utterly bereft
of culture and civility.
See how they run, scuttling, scurrying,
scrabbling over each other to reach the top
where poisoned honey comb is stored
and the insatiable queen awaits;
they all knew what they thought they wanted;
now it's too late to change.

Dry wings and exo-skeletons,
for inside there's only mush,
crumble where they fell and blow away.
The competitive samsaric race
of hymenoptera and humans
is finished.

The wise say that samsara,
the world of suffering, and
blissful nirvana are the same,
one seen through the distorting
eye of ignorance, the other in
the light of eternity.
Sophisticated despair
(or existential *Angst*) is samsaric,
nirvana is the realisation
that nothing is ultimately wrong
save our perception of it.

35
1968-1970

A golden down showering
or maybe upsurging of grace,
gentle at first unrealised
eventually touching and changing
almost everyone, even resisters
through a thickening of clam shell
obduracy, even the silly ones
who grew like weeds then flopped
and denied it all forgetting dawn
in the fat feasts of afternoon.

We feel things quickly
understand them slowly.
I felt I couldn't do and didn't want
the things I had enjoyed,
knew I'd been wrong on almost everything –
the way I taught, development,
race, sex, the lot.
I'd carried an old man, spiritually
constipated, alert for ego-slight,
very heavy although
completely insubstantial.
When he fell off I fairly bounced along
happy and light but wits
not yet grasping what had really happened.

Much later it came clear:
we all are one,
not mistrustfully separate.
That's fact not metaphysical
conceit. Then came another kind
of revelation in this
perpetual reve – revolution:
now I must turn the laser on myself
to light up and to burn away the false.

36
The Pawns

A most distasteful task, telling
The Powindahs* they must leave the hills,
Their immemorial summer home.
Riding unhappily through the empty
Mountains (expecting also to fall off
At any minute)
Eventually we reached the upland valley
Where black felt tents are pitched, hobbled
Camels, flocks of goats and fat tailed sheep
Stippling the bare hill sides.
To greet us, an avenue of men
Blazing away with rifles as
We pass between them. Amazed that I
Am still on my frightened horse, we reach the camp.
There greeted by the fine-robed elders
And led into the largest tent to dine.
Upon my left, the senior *malik*,
Fierce of men but gravely courteous;
Upon my right, somewhat dandified,
Tiny pearl handled pistol in his belt
(Others having more emphatic weapons)
A younger man who talks of high society
In Kabul and Lahore, a cut above,
He seems to hint, these tough
Illiterate tribesmen.

After our feast, the dancing. Young men,
Black turbans cast aside, start slowly circling,
Then faster, faster, broad swords slicing
And flashing, long hair aswirl;
The older warriors leap out, spin
At the circle's centre, firing wildly
With sub-machine guns while the lonely hills
Reverberate. My prissy neighbour
Joining in, primps from his cushioned seat,
Lets fly – 'poop poop' – with his toy pistol.

At last, reluctantly, the business.
The government of Pakistan, I say,
Objects to these annual incursions
Into its territory. The Afghan
Nomads and their flocks introduce
Diseases, the animals eat too much
Pakistani grass, the men smuggle
(Other objections I have now repressed);
So they must go.

I hate to give this most ungracious news
To hospitable hosts.
The *malik* looked unhappy, his ferocity
Dimmed by puzzled resignation.
'This is a world', he said, 'we do not understand;
Pakistan, Afghanistan, national boundaries,
These mean nothing to us. We only know
The mountains are our people's home,
Were so for centuries before such
New-fangled notions were invented'.

I returned with passionate and reasoned
Pleas on their behalf; all turned down.
Ironically the Powindahs
Were later on reprieved,
But not through humanity;
Through the wholly anti-human
Calculus of great-power politics
And spheres of strategic interest
That turn people into pawns.

Some years on, for similar expediencies
In altered international alignments,
They were again ejected.

Later yet they all came back as refugees
Sacrificed once more as other
Kings and queens fought out the game.

* This name for Afghan nomads is etymologically related to the English word wander.

37
Tweedledum and Tweedledee

President A said 'we are a
Peace loving people who honour
Virginity and motherhood
(Sequentially of course);
We would take any reasonable step
To end this fearful conflict,
But our enemies,
Infamous and brutal warmongers,
Aim only to destroy us. They reject
Any sensible peace initiatives,
Leaving us no choice
But to fight on until
Victory is finally achieved'.

President B said 'we are
Dedicated to the quest for
Peace with justice.
We revere marriage and the family;
We long to end this ghastly war
But every move we make is thwarted
By those bastards who want
Only to wipe us out.
This gives us no alternative
But to fight on until
Victory is finally achieved'.

President A said 'our soldiers
Are well disciplined and patriotic.
They respect the Geneva convention
But will fight implacably
Until they conquer.
B's men, however, are a rabble,
Treacherous as weasels
And bloodthirsty as ferrets'.

President B said ‘our brave men
Are matchless in their
Military skill, chivalry
And moral commitment;
They will overwhelm the cruel
And cowardly brigands whom A
Calls his army’.

After a few drinks late at night
President A lets down his hair,
‘I don’t know how the hell
We can get out of this
God awful mess.
I really feel that time is running out.
We’re doing badly on the northern front
And Moscow haven’t come up with
The help they promised us;
I really don’t know where
We’ll turn to next’.

In comparable circumstances
President B said ‘shit,
The bloody Pentagon have let us down;
They guaranteed us
Military aid
But now the sodding Senate’s
Voted against it.
I really can’t think what
We’ll do instead’.

When A and B were separately asked
If they had reached a point
Where they would seriously consider
Negotiating a settlement,
They made similar responses.

President A said ‘I have
Been ready all the time;
I would sign a truce tomorrow
If I could trust B

As far as I could throw him.
But how can I believe his protestations
When he's dropping napalm
On our villages?
It simply doesn't square'.

President B said 'of course.
But it takes two to tango.
Whatever A says about wanting peace
Is utterly at variance with his acts.
The lousy hypocrite is using
Every dirty trick in the book,
Dumdum bullets, booby trapped bodies, gas, the lot.
How can I have confidence in anything
He does or says?'

Since a certain mutual trust
Is necessary for successful negotiation,
It was suggested that
Reciprocating gestures might be made
By each president, to inspire
Confidence in the other.
For example, A might stop
Bombing B's cities;
B might order a limited
Cease fire in the northern sector
Where his boys were doing rather well.
Such steps might convince
Each leader of the other's
Sincerity and peaceable intentions, thus
Lowering tensions
That would otherwise impede
A constructive exchange.

President A said 'I see your point,
But if we stop the bombing
Their morale will improve,
Their factories produce more war matériel,
Their communication system
Return to normal.

So, no. A good idea, but not for us,
Not at this stage;
I really couldn't trust them
to play fair.'

President B said 'I'm all for
Lowering tension,
But not at the cost of military
Disadvantage. Those buggers
Would simply take the opportunity
To bring up reinforcements
And improve their positions;
They wouldn't keep to their side
of the bargain'.

So they went on mauling, mutilating
And slaughtering each other with ever
Increasing mindless ferocity,
Having of course gained access,
Many being eager to assist them,
To fresh supplies of arms.
The young men died miserable and unready
In the swamps, deserts and jungles,
The mothers and the virgins were bombed
Or shattered by cannon
Fire from the waspish planes, and
When their villages were overrun,
Raped, slashed and left to die.
As for family life, it became
One protracted funeral.

After a few months
(Or may be it was years)
Another period of exhausted stalemate.

President A, a trifle out of sorts,
Then finally agreed to sue for peace,
But before his message could be brought to B
His troops had gained an unforeseen success.
Changing his mind

He cried 'I'll never yield
A single hectare of our sacred soil.
We shall fight on until
Victory is finally achieved.'
(He then proceeded to discredit
The messenger who had witnessed
His momentary weakness.)

The next time around it was
President B who threw in the sponge.
But, like A, unexpectedly doing
Better in the battle,
Caught it before it fell.
He then promptly reaffirmed
His complete commitment to the
Achievement of final victory.

And so they go on and on
Throughout the planet,
The many As and Bs,
Trapped in the pride and fear,
The paranoid suspicion of each other
That spreads to infect their people
Until all are sick of a fever
That's burning up the world.

38
The Unorthodox Wool Carder

Baghdad, Anno Domini 922,
That is the year of the Hijra 309,
A Sufi named Al Hillaj,
Which means the carder of wool,
Who happened to be a devotee of the Prophet Isa,
The Lord of the Spirit and the Word,
Whom Christians call Jesus,
Was, like him, crucified for heresy,
Which is often indistinguishable
From political subversion.
His crime: to have stated repeatedly
'Ana' l Haqq, that is 'I am the Truth'.

He wasn't claiming to be God,
But it sounded like it, at least so thought
The fanatical elders who judged him.
What he meant, he wrote in *Kitab al Tawasin*,*
Was that he should be seen as a sign
Of God, manifesting his truth,
Which is indeed always available to those
Who seek it inwardly with loving reverence.

But the orthodox, then and now, detest all mystics
Who see by an inner light –
Illuminati, charismatics, enthusiasts,
Even the generally law-abiding
And respectable modern Quakers.

Those in whom the spirit works
With iconoclastic unpredictability
(In this particular case the Sufis) threaten
Order, stability, certainty,
Established hierarchy and vested interests
Both secular and clerical.
They certainly have no place

In any society where wealth is
Considered the gauge of human worth,
In which millionaires alone are considered
Fit to run the nation and in which
The arms trade is a major source of profit.

No wonder Al Hillaj, rejecting
Recantation as blasphemy,
Was condemned to death.

Arriving at the place of execution,
Seeing the cross and nails, he stopped to pray,
Ending with these words:
'Forgive these men for killing me,
Out of mistaken fervour,
In your name. If you had blessed them
With the knowledge vouchsafed me
They would have done differently;
Had you withheld from me what you revealed
I would have been spared this tribulation.
But praise to you, oh God, and glory
In all you do and everything you will'.

Whereupon one named the Herdsman,
Furious at the heretic's presumption,
Struck him down, smashing his face.

Then he was scourged and nailed up to die.

* There is no generally agreed translation for this title. Judging by the text it might be something like *Essay on Self-unification*.

39
Celebration of Kindness

We should all celebrate kindness,
I don't just mean the generous
and pleasant actions that so often
surprise and delight, but as universal
impulse. We're kind by nature,
loving to love and show it. Unkindness
is distortion, a sickness to be cured by
love as anyone can demonstrate.
Mother love is archetypal kindness,
so let's all start by celebrating mothers.

40
Old Men

Old men, it seems, are supposed
To sit around dreaming of the past.
I say, being one of them, this is crap.
For one thing it makes you sad
To no purpose
Remembering people and places
You won't see again, and
Things you won't do any more.
If you reminisce aloud you
Alienate surviving friends,
If inwardly, you addle and confuse the mind.

Don't either try to play the wise
Old man, you'll only make an ass of yourself
And embarrass the young (who also make fools
Of themselves, but it's not so obvious
As senile folly);
Recognise that you neither know what they
Are talking about, nor understand
Their outlook on life,
Just accept that it's different but OK
For them. Equally don't act young.
There's nothing sillier than
An old bugger trying to keep up
With his juniors physically
Let alone, God help us,
Amorously.

And never try to hog the conversation
With obsolete opinions,
Tedious anecdotes and outworn jokes;
In general, just try to shut up.
All these things distract you
From what you should be doing.

And what, you crossly ask, is that?

Look, I answer, you're now in a new phase;
Change gear.
Don't grate along in third, move into
Overdrive.

But you just said...

No, the point is that old men
Try to keep in top when
The road is too steep. Hence
Heart attacks, cancer, depression
And cranky bad temper.
No; choose a different road, a different gear.
Remember you are free. No need at all
To make a show, to keep up or look young,
Be witty or profound.
These are all obstacles to *being*.

Being what, for heaven's sake?

Being nothing,
That's the reward when outer work is done,
Pension arrives regularly, family's settled.
Life's complete.
The boasts, the dreams, the attempts at humour
Wasteful and unnecessary. They only
Separate you from the void of being,
Of being nothing, nothing, nothing,
No thing.

Except who you fundamentally are.

41

When Jesus Spoke

When Jesus spoke the light shone,
The blind could see, the sick were well,
But the bishop saying the selfsame words
Opened the gate of hell.

Plague creeps unnoticed through the land,
Film grows over bright eyes,
Tongues seeming to speak truthfully,
Tell only lies.

Our worth is measured by success
In games where the losers are broken
And winners taste hectic delights
Before their sentence is spoken.

Hearts shrivel and falter in their beat
Lacking love's blood;
When we see the gate gape foul before us
The bishop smoothly mentions God.

42
Pacifism

For pacifist read coward, appeaser,
Traitor, one who skulks at home
While others defend him, someone
Soft on Russia and other obnoxious
Regimes, who wants to placate
The wicked without standing up for
Britain against her enemies, unpatriotic,
A subverter of the values
That made our country great,
Who puts foreigners first, a communist,
At best a weak and silly fool
Misled by insidious propaganda,
The tool of lefties, Trots and others
Eager to humble and destroy us.
It means people like me, an unhealthy
Influence on the young, unreliable,
Furtive, a bit mysterious, up to no good,
A betrayer of his class, disgrace to his school,
Soft on serious academic standards.
The least hostile critics are just scornful,
'Why waste your time? There always have been wars,
It's human nature; Freud said so'.

Whew! The load of shit poured out on peaceniks
Passes belief. I had naively thought
That work for peace would be respected, save
Perhaps by a few retired colonels
(Who, knowing war, in fact, are often friendlier),
And save when pacifists themselves are full
Of anger, selfrighteousness and arrogance
As can be the case with anyone
Supporting causes less for their own worth
Than for personal fulfilment,
But it's more noticeably inappropriate
When the cause is good. I keep explaining

That being a pacifist just means seeing
That war is a rotten way to resolve
Human differences, wasteful,
Inefficient, bringing death and anguish
To many thousands quite unrelated
To the quarrel and seldom leading to results
Even the aggressors would have wanted.
But of course the root of pacifism
Is not that war is futile but is wrong.
It negates the basic reality
That all is one and humanity a whole,
Try though we may to subdivide it.
Belief in the use of war is heresy
Now become horribly orthodox.

But pacifists are not just complainers;
They constantly search for and assay
Alternative means of
Untangling dangerous disputes
And methods of nonviolent resistance
To oppressors and invaders,
Ways of frustrating without killing
Them, especially without
The anger of the heart which smears
With hatred any neutral act.

This can be perilous work, demanding the discipline,
Organisation and courage of an army
Ready to face death without retaliating.
Now what's so cowardly and traitorous about that?

The evidence suggests we tend to have
Some addiction to the idea of war.
Most soldiers know, as General Sherman said,
'Its glory is all moonshine...war is hell',
But others feel its terrible attraction;
They think there's something wrong with those who don't,
They smell different to witch-hunting snouts.
Paradoxically we talk of peace a lot,
But what we mean is stable benefits

Preserved for our special group,
Usually at the expense of those less favoured.

Thus we crow as the emasculation of unions
Brings peace and prosperity (we hope)
To shareholders, or smashing the Argies
Sets the old lion roaring croakily,
Delighting those whose sons
Were not incinerated.

Whence this streak of violence within us?
Our animal inheritance, perhaps,
But feral violence is usually functional
Serving a purpose our excesses don't.
It stems more likely from our fundamental
Illusion of separateness, of difference
And so, too often, superiority to the other
Nation, tribe, family, cult or individual,
Loftiness laced with fear that justifies
Our killing with words like patriotism
Giving to it a lurid spurious glamour.

But truth is never totally concealed
Even from those most deeply deluded.
Along with their belligerence there is
A pitiful yearning for a perfect state;
For peace in fact, but say it not aloud.

43
Eternal Life

Humble that stubborn heart,
obey the Lord,
be pure, acquire merit,
bind yourself tightly with
the golden chain of virtue,
thus save your soul and earn
a blissful life in heaven
when you die.

If otherwise your sentence is
a term in purgatory
or if beyond redemption
the flames forever –
a most imperious
incentive to be good,
like it or not,

Thus most religions con us
(and usually themselves).
The 'immortal soul'
exhorted and admonished
by their priests
is just another word for ego, 'I',
a skein of evanescent selves,
the false identity.

When we are dead the particles
of consciousness that body
ties together (and which create
our hells while yet we live) –
this salad of opinions, that
passionate attachment, this
piece of quirkiness, all these
illusions of a separate self
then fly apart,

their forces are dispersed
to other uses or to
other bodies.

But if we gain salvation
or enlightenment
we see the 'I' and all the rest
as fading phantoms.
The sole foundation
now revealed is Mind,
the glorious Void, the Absolute,
which was, will be and always is
before and after
life and death.

44

Agape?

My friend the guerrilla leader
had a plane blown up
killing some twenty holiday makers,
British, French and Japanese,
all irrelevant to the struggle.
By chance the fuse, or whatever
new device they now employ, was short,
otherwise the plane
would have exploded in mid-air
killing the whole lot.
This act was aimed to draw attention
to the cause, as certainly it did,
most adversely.

Of course this murderer isn't still my friend?
Why not?
Below the mad conditioning of oppression
the essence of his being still survives;
surely compassion and attempts to show
a gentler way are of much greater worth
than self-righteous hatred if,
tortured by the suffering of his people
his violence repeats
what has been done to them.
That's how it goes:
the death of one small girl over Greece
leads to revenge in which another
dies in Tripoli;*
and show me any cause worth
slaughtered children.

Ironically the acronym of my friend's group
spells love
but of the secular not spiritual kind:
perhaps eventually this may change.

* In 1986 a bomb exploded in an American airliner flying over Greece, blowing a hole in the hull. Several people, including a little girl were sucked through this hole and fell to their deaths. In retaliation the American airforce, with British connivance, launched an attack on Tripoli in which, among others, a baby adopted daughter of Colonel Qadhafi was also killed.

45
The Bureaucrat and the Refugees

Urbane bureaucrat, tight-lipped tight-assed simulacrum of a man
ordering the fate of humanity by the standards of Whitehall and
Wimbledon, pawning your heart for the price of a bowler hat,

how serious your study of the regulations (and their political
implications) applying to aliens (undesirable) and immigrants
(illegal),

how pure your existential joy in completing the deportation order to
consign some lesser being, certainly foreign probably black,
to torture, detention camp or some comparable form of extinction.

Loosen those lips, that sphincter, redeem that heart. Imagine with
the inner eye reopened, the multitude of fugitives.

Consider:

the throngs of dispossesed criss-crossing each other's trails through-
out the world, the ravening hunters ever closing in with yelps of
pleasure to drag them from their ricketty shelters,

to strip them, dowse them with petrol, dance around excited,
masturbating; then light a match,

to slam them into cattle wagons, feed them with salted fish, deny
them water and dump the survivors in a frozen wilderness,

to hurl them into the bloody gob and rotting teeth of war;

and consider what they fled from:

the cold appraisal of the secret police, the rule
of tyrants, the hatred aroused by just being what they are;

and consider kindly their hope:

for what you fine fellow have always taken for granted – not of course for central heating, package holidays, new cars, luxurious meals, but enough to eat, basic medicine, freedom to say more or less what they want and to do more or less what they like; to have, without frills, a normal life expectancy.

46
In the Supermarket

Ravenous but never satisfied,
Yearning for the food of experience
They cannot swallow,
Roam the hungry ghosts
Desperately scanning the shelves
For what always eludes them.

Occasionally a Rolls drives up
Full of glittering people,
Too happy and healthy in their high estate
To realise mortality.
They bray to each other across the aisles
(As though we were not there)
Of smoked salmon they forgot to buy
At Fortnum and Mason's.

There are also the animals,
Stoking up with beef and booze,
Snuffling humourless in troughs of greed
And lusty excitement,
Oblivious of all else.

Once I met and fled from
Past dairy products to safety in bread and biscuits,
A hell-being, cavernous eyes half hid,
Cold mouth smirking, prowling for victims,
Consumed by thoughts of rape, torture and slow death
(And incidentally doing a weekend shop).

There were also human beings.
They carried shopping bags,
Made sensible purchases,
Talked in a friendly, helpful fashion
And went home calmly, knowing who they were.
    Is it true what the Tibetans say,
    That fully human birth is rare?

According to Tibetan Buddhism there are six states of existence: *pretas*, insatiably hungry ghosts; *devas* and *asuras*, demi-gods and titans who are too well endowed to confront suffering; *naraks*, hell-beings reaping the consequences of evil acts; animals; and human beings, who suffer greatly, but have the capacity to gain release from suffering, and so to help others to do so, through enlightenment. Some would say, however, that these categories are merely metaphors for human psychological types. Not many of us, they imply, are completely human.

47
Coincidence

An airport worker was ripped
By the blast when my friend's
Guerrilla band blew up the plane.
After a spell in hospital
He went home to convalesce.

When sufficiently recovered
He set out for the capital
To receive compensation
For his injuries.

But he never got it;
The bus on which he was
Travelling was also blown up,
By another guerrilla group,
And this time he was killed.

Some called this a most unlucky
Chance. Others said his karma
Must have run out. I'd only add
It's the sort of miserable
Thing we must expect in war.

48
Choices

The devastating clear light of awareness
Occasionally strikes. Our spirit
Blinks, draws back. Impossible to think
We should accept it, giving up everything.
Lucky there's a less demanding light,
Restful, cloudy yellow or dull red,
Not penetrating and challenging;
Turning to this, we send off our fat cheques
To Oxfam.

The teaching* says that always after death
The clear light of reality appears;
Another chance, but as in life
Usually rejected out of fear;
It comes again, again, but still we can't
Abandon cosy havens of
Habitual illusion,
The comfortably murky glow of lies.

But every time we choose the dimmer beam
Our chance to reach enlightenment grows less.
At length we find our refuge in some womb,
Issuing to start the tedious cycle
Once again.

* In the *Tibetan Book of the Dead*, Bardo Thödol.

49
Oh, Bangladesh

The Bengalis of East Pakistan,
Now Bangladesh, were charming and
Sensitive people, much addicted
To poetry and song. In right season
They drifted down the great waterways
In elegant boats bedecked with flowers,
Making music, picnicking
And in general being innocently happy.

Later their ghastly suffering (over a million died
At the insane insensate hands,
Calloused with contemptuous arrogance,
Of their overlords) seemed all the worse
For their harmless peacefulness.

But after this experience they learned fast.
In the last sixteen years
They have certainly joined the club.
Membership qualification: butcher
Your leaders, preferably with their families,
Supporters and in fact anyone you dislike
Having first contrived to attach
A derogatory ideological label.
Then butcher the butchers, promising
Endlessly postponed elections.

Additional qualification:
Designate some minority group,
In this case the Buddhist Chakma tribe
(Incidentally the most appealing and
Talented people I ever met)
As terrorists, a fashionable term, conveniently
Legitimising any barbarity
And, of course, eliciting at last
A comparable response to justify

The whining ferocity of the
Burners of villages, rapers of women,
Bold slayers of children
In the cause of freedom and democracy.

So three cheers, Bangladesh, you're doing fine,
You've put away childish things,
The boat trips, songs, the merriment
And joined the real world. But still you lack
A certain sophistication in the
Techniques of torture, of political
Mendacity, of dedicated ruthlessness.
Perhaps you haven't entirely
Eradicated a trace of softness
That goes with poetry, art, all that stuff.
But work on it and you'll make the top league yet.

Meanwhile upon the rivers leaking boats
Bearing withered garlands, broken sitars,
Like the discarded soul of Bangladesh,
Drift aimlessly away.

50
Lies

We should complete that crack
About lies, damned lies and statistics
By adding statements made by public figures,
Especially those that deny responsibility,
Shift the guilt, smear their opponents,
Or extol their own wisdom, generosity,
Compassion for the poor
Or concern for anything
Not affecting themselves
Such as public transport, state education
And the national health service.

How refreshing it would be if,
Just occasionally, they admitted being wrong,
However slightly. But perhaps
It's better not, for if they did then I
Might be inclined to swallow their next lie.

51
Puzzles

Mullah Nasruddin,*
one of the first recorded lateral thinkers,
burnt incense and lit candles in his garden.
When asked why, he answered
'to keep tigers away'.
His friends said 'you're daft,
there are no tigers around here'.
'Just so', said Nasruddin,
'that only shows the virtue
of my methods'.

Lady Euphorbia Pluffingham
is not frightened of tigers
but disease.
She had herself innoculated against
cholera, typhus and bubonic plague
before taking a weekend trip
to Bournemouth.
Her friends said 'you're daft,
you can't catch those illnesses
in that place'.

But she did; all of them.
From her sickbed she triumphantly
if weakly riposted
'now you must admit that I was right
to have those jabs;
its just a pity that the vaccine
wasn't stronger'.

Now what would Nasruddin have made of that?

* Mullah Nasruddin was a character created, probably around the twelfth century, by the dervishes. The Nasruddin stories are at one level quirky jokes, at another startling paradoxes and mind-twising conundrums, at yet another revelations of spiritual reality. Their effect, and their purpose, is similar to that of a Zen *koan;* they stop us in our tracks and force us to reassess our conventional view of reality, and ourselves in relation to it.

52
On Going To The Wars

Usually they don't know –
best keep these things a little dark –
although a few wish quietly
god speed and safe return.

Preoccupied with routine chores,
visa, packing, travellers cheques,
I grin and shrug, pretending calm
but inwardly hear nothing save
the hurrying hours hammer home
the lid on my life.

53
Massacre

Every one was killed, I said,
One hundred and twenty eight
Market women and their babies
By a cluster bomb, or whatever they're called,
Exploding near ground level.

He sighed, this decent young man,
A prayer book on the desk, a photo
Of his mistress and *his* baby,
A most reluctant butcher
Snared in the trap of violence.
'I'm grieved, they were my people, but perhaps
This tragedy will help to end the war'.

How might that be?

'The fearful consequences of
Rebellion will be obvious, they will then
Lay down their arms, an awful but
Perhaps necessary lesson'.

Not so, I said.
They learned another lesson, that all the
Propaganda about genocide was true,
Why else kill those poor innocents,
Not military targets, not them.
They don't understand the problems
Of a mercenary pilot,
Scared stiff, at high speed, tree top level,
Jettisoning his load anywhere –
By ill chance on a market place.
No, all they see, the splattered bodies,
All they know, their leaders spoke the truth;
You mean to wipe them out.

Better to die fighting than to wait
For massacre; let's take as many
Of them with us as we can.

Yes, that's what they are saying.

He understood and nodded sombrely.

54

Our Nature

There's some good in everyone;
boring old cliché and not true anyway.
Everyone is good, but some so screwed up
they can't express it
so it comes out as evil.
I don't mean those unfortunates
(all of us at times) are
necessarily crazy or neurotic
in any clinical sense (though some are),
simply dislocated from the truth
that love and generous wisdom
alone bring happiness,
the sense of being one with life.

But why do we go so wrong?
Well, you can take your pick of theories –
ethological, psychoanalytic,
let alone theological – original sin,
for example, *maya*, *ghafla*,*
or the ignorance that Buddhists blame.

But speculation's fruitless,
better to dwell on what is positive:
the Mahayana knowledge that we are,
not have, mark you, but *are*,
the Buddha nature;
Ibn Arabi: 'the perfect being is one who knows
the sole existence is that of God';
Jesus: 'the kingdom of God is within you' and
'it extends throughout the land but men see it not'.

Great beings have ever taught the unity
of all things, of creator and creation.
Our only task: to recognise the fact.

* *Maya:* the Sanscrit for illusion, a term much used in Hindu philosophy. *Ghafla:* the Arabic for forgetfulness, a word used by the Sufis to describe our failure to recognise or remember the divine reality.

55
Snails

I love snails.
Their advance I find stately and noble,
Their stalked eyes both innocent and jaunty.
I'm not, however, quite so keen
On what they do to my vegetables,
The tender bean, lettuce or parsley.
Don't blame them, mind, it's their natural right
To chew up any tasty leaf that's going,
They don't know about horticulture
Or land ownership.
Recently, lifting some concrete slabs
By the compost heap,
I discovered hundreds underneath.
Big and small, they were stuck
To each other or the slabs
In a most cosy and charming fashion.

Touched by this happy sight,
Yet trembling for the delicate plants
Nearby, I wondered what to do.
Impossible, of course, to kill the snails
Or excessively to incommode them,
Equally so to leave them where they were,
The shortest slime trail from the lettuce bed,
Unneighbourly to drop them over
The fence and too near anyway.

So I detached them as gently as I could,
Put them in a Sainsbury's plastic bag
And took them to the nearby wood.
There in a zone of succulent new growth
(Though possibly less dainty than my seedlings)
I found them a new home
And left them with my blessings.

56

The Toys of War

Crouched in the belly of the empty
Plane (it had been full of dried fish
And sugar), backs against the fuselage,
We flew from the beleaguered air strip,
Tracer bullets curling lazily
But lethally towards us,
The battle furious in the jungle below.
Then flung around in a bucketing storm
And landing thankfully at dawn
On Fernando Po
Where cocoa made with condensed milk
Smoothed out hungry tensions.

Among us
A woman from London and her son;
Skin hung on her arms in yellow flaps
(Protein deficiency and prolonged starvation).
The lad, about eleven, cheerful
And considerate, helping her, the father
Left behind.

She said: My son was in the navy,
A few speed boats,
Machine guns bolted to the decks,
Zooming through the mangrove swamps
And shooting up the enemy.
He fought well.
But a youngster, even if a sailor,
Still needs toys.
He had one, a Federal soldier's head,
Kept it in a bucket which for fun
He'd swing around or hoist up on the mast.
Paused and considered:
But it's not the proper life for a little boy.

We agreed that this was so.

57
Meetings

Lifetimes, it often seems to me,
lost voicing our opinions,
deriding or refuting those of others;
nasty things, those opinions,
great adjuncts of the ego,
showing how smart we are and how profound,
how experienced and worldly wise
or, according to the context,
how spiritual.
My opinion becomes part of me,
attack it at your peril,
I'll take it as a personal affront
and if I'm incontestably proved wrong
it's like damage to a prized possession;
my identity,
the false self I love so utterly,
is really mutilated
requiring psycho-plastic surgery.

So a meeting is a fairly tense affair;
there's more to win or lose
than a debating point.
We're all too busy working out our speeches,
so logical, so eloquent and witty,
to listen to what others have to say.
Ingenious and appropriate ideas,
along with plenteous platitude and drivel,
are voiced unheard.

Eventually when everyone is tired,
keen to get home to tea,
being satisfied they've had their say
and said it well,
someone repeats a wise proposal
made at the very outset of the meeting.
'That's right', we all agree. 'I wonder why
no one suggested this before;
we could have finished several hours ago'.

58
Pigeons

While waiting for a bus, thoughts
somewhat improbably arose
about the Holy Spirit.
Was it always available,
making itself known when the heart is cleansed;
or is it capricious as *The Acts*
suggest, like lightning striking
unpredictably?

Suddenly came a pigeon flock
swooping veering slanting
through the air powerful
precise masters of the sky
skimming the ground then
sweeping upwards quite unlike
the portly waddlers of
Trafalgar Square.

That's maybe how it is, I thought, recalling
the French speak of the Holy Ghost
as the *Sainte Pigeon*.

59

Life and Death

Why worry about death,
Nothing can really die
Except the unmourned ego.
The energies and shreds of mind
And body change, persist and flow
Onward. Only deluded I,
Yearning for permanence, can
Disintegrate, dissolve, die
And by its vanishing reveal
Life's blazing panoply and show
That death's a lie.

60
Sketches of Inequality

During the floods I joined a rescue team
(I don't know why they let me come
Along, if I'd been hurt there would have
Been hell to pay). We pulled down houses
Now become dangerous, shifted
People from islands soon to be
Submerged. Their hutments, never
Dry, were now awash, mud walls crumbling,
Cardboard, thatch, corrugated iron
Falling pitifully apart,
Shit floating on the muddy water
(Proof of the fibre diet we
Pay a lot for). Nevertheless
These were their homes. We rescued them;
Where they went next was someone
Else's business.
                                        I drove to the suburb
From the slum, showered, changed, had
A stiff gin, feeling pretty good.

* * * *

The governor of this province,
Malik Amir Mohammad, Khan of Kalabagh,
Was an interesting mixture;
Both shrewd industrialist and
Mediaeval despot;
His manner courteous, very
Anglicised (he knew all the
Best county families),
But never let his several
Wives be seen. His estates
Covered the area of about
One third of Somerset.
He admired the English landlords
Because, he said, they understood
How to control their peasants.

He wasn't too bad at it himself;
He told a friend with peasant-trouble
(They objected to his hunting
Parties trampling their crops)
'Mine complained once, but I just put
Fifty-seven of them underground'
(A delicate euphemism
For arson, beating up and murder)
'There's been no hint of trouble ever since'.[1]

* * * *

Scrambling down from the Shandur Pass
To the cluster of poor tents below
The rotting glaciers of Buni Zom,[2]
We found a seemingly hostile
Reception, but soon discovered
They were only angrily sad;
Being themselves starving, they
Could not entertain us as
They would have wished.
We said no matter, we weren't hungry
And spent a happy evening with them.
They generously lit a fire – not
Much wood at ten thousand feet in
The Hindu Kush.
I passed round cigarettes (smoked then)
And we all had Kashgar soup – we'd got
The packet in Hunza; it was foul.

They were starving, they told,
Because their overlords taxed
Them in kind, their labour to maintain
The tracks, and a tithe
Of their frugal crops.
Thus their own supplies were
Invariably used up some weeks
Before the next harvest.
The old and the young often died
Of malnutrition or of blockages
Caused by eating grass, their only food.

Surely there must be something you can do?

No, nothing. If we protest,
Their men will come to beat or shoot us.
It has always been like this; the rich
Oppress the poor; the poor suffer;
It is the will of God.

We left in murky dawn like ghosts,
Beside the glacier, down the empty valley
Towards the distant castle, barbaric
And magnificent, of the overlords
Who madly tried to kill us.

1. But his own fate had the grim justice of a Greek tragedy. His eldest son, crazed by the father's contemptuous rejection of his plea to be allowed to marry a Swiss woman, shot him dead.

2. A mountain of 21,000 feet.

61
Suspense

Suddenly they broke off contact,
friendliness changed silently to silence –
no visitors, no phone calls, nothing.
We waited wondering, in that alien town.

Peace makers don't endear themselves
to everyone.
Even when leaders want a settlement
dissident fanatics or big business
may hope for better bargains
continuing the struggle,
so do their best to bugger up the deal.
A quite effective way is killing
mediators. We recalled
several of our friends vanished
or found torn with bullet wounds.

Wondering, we waited.

62

Mandala

Sad little streets, restrained, Victorian,
The letter box gory in its place
At the junction of Underhill
And Belvoir, sodden laurels dankly
Sheltering myriad woodlice.
The sixty three bus turns down Melford
Between the poles of Kings Cross
And Crystal Palace
Carrying its nameless burden
Of hidden lives behind draped lace.

Adjust the spirits lens; the mandala
Comes in focus, the divine space.
The streets channels for cosmic winds,
The letter box a beacon of delight,
The furtive fox rummaging my compost bin
Now the messenger of grace;
The thundering buses, wrathful deities
Expelling ignorance,
Each house a living face.
Brave light dissolves the fog
Changing shapeless scurrying people
Into Bodhisattvas
Strolling in this holy place.

63

Ecology Then and Now

Topping the last hill,
even the camels weary and athirst,
we saw, quavering in the heat and biscuit dry,
the once great city.

The roof still on some houses,
pitch in the broken stubs
of terracotta torches;
who would have thought a thousand years
had passed since they were lived in
and the flares were lit.

Along the arid valley floor
the fossil stumps of trees
showed how it must have been.
But no life now.

The Romans hadn't done much better
(ably abetted by the goats)
than ourselves.
But here's the difference:
while now we know precisely
what we're doing
and never give a damn except
about quick profits,
presumably they'd never heard
about ecology.

64
Action

We are more powerful than we know; everything we do, say or think has an effect; it sends ripples to the edge of eternity, interacting unpredictably with an infinite number of other actions, words and thoughts and with increasingly unforeseeable results.

So the effects of our actions are largely beyond our control. Any happening they may influence has multiple causes that can never be unravelled; the contribution of what we did is as hard to assess as that of a single strand in a rope.

I once thought I had done something having a good and clear result. A friend and I ran the blockade bringing cash to buy food for a beleaguered and starving people. Learning later that thousands had thereby been fed for many months, I thought: well, that's very different from the usual uncertainty whether our work ever benefits anyone at all; now, because of what we did, people live who would otherwise be dead.

How naive!

Our dollars had been changed to worthless local currency, then flown out to purchase weapons. Thus was the war prolonged, the famine continued, while many more were killed by the newly acquired guns and bullets.

Once we tried for years to arrange peace talks: failed. Eventually the war ended by battle rather than by negotiation. But instead of the expected vengeful carnage, miraculous reconciliation. The victors, forgetting fostered hatred, took the vanquished to their hearts, healed and fed them.

Our efforts, we were told, had helped to change their vision from one blurred by anger to one cleared by compassion.

So, greatly oversimplifying, what had seemed success was a failure; and failure a success. But since then, on what strange and unexpected shores have those ripples broken; to what joy or suffering have they contributed?

The lesson I learned: forget about results. If things appear to have gone wrong, don't yield to grief; nor to self-congratulation if they seem to turn out well. You don't know; the real effects of our actions remain hidden.

So why do anything?

There's no option; even to do nothing is to act, perhaps in the most worthless of ways. We must have faith that if we purify our hearts making our motives more compassionate, what we do will strengthen, unimaginably, the great forces that can save humanity.

But if, instead of being led by love, we are concerned with the part we personally play, and crave the gratification of seeming success, we shall weaken them.

65
Straw

It has been recorded that when Thomas
Aquinas had finished his great work,
Summa Theologica,
He put his head into his hands saying
'Compared with what I inwardly have seen
This is no more valuable than straw'.

Although I've seen and written infinitely less,
I can say much the same.
These attempts at poetry are merely
Shadows, at best symbols of a truth
I dimly sense but can't convey to you.
The incidents I write about, the
Conflicts, agonies, confusions
Are bad dreams of humanity that light
Will dissipate. The efforts to express
A teaching or philosophy, mere echoes
Of a sacred mantra distorted by
The craggy cliffs of ignorance.
The brain in which these fantasies arise,
A thought machine in which electric
Impulses leap wild and uncontrolled
From neuron to neuron firing fresh
Illusions; but all of this breaks down
From cell to molecule to atom, then to
The universe of sub-atomic space,
Pure energy, no shape, nothing
But the void, splendid and enigmatic,
From which we come and into which we go,
Eternally and ceaselessly recurrent.
These immaterial hands holding this helpless
Head are similarly phantoms. But from
Annihilation I'm built up once more
To *think* I think, to write, to act, to feel,
Frustrated that there's always something which
I never grasp but can't stop trying to.

And so from day to day and birth to birth
We must go on, but sometimes sensing
That beyond the straw there must be grain,
The growing germ, the very source of life.

66
Moving House

Joints getting creaky
eyes and hearing, well, mediocre
blood pressure unstable
too many brain cells not functioning
properly or dead
in short, body not too good.
Worse still, mind cluttered with
pointless ideas and memories
likes and dislikes
accumulated junk
of seventy one years.

Prepare for a new start
discard what's ripe for leaving
and tidy up a bit
dust polish and repair anything
that might be good to take
to the next home.

67
Journey to the Centre

All paths lead to the centre.

They are always long and arduous, the farther you go the harder.

If you travel staunchly you may be rewarded with occasional pleasant resting places, but don't mistake these for the centre; once you are refreshed you must continue.

Though the routes all have the same destination it may be wiser to choose one which begins by passing through familiar terrain,

But if you follow it properly, not with preconceptions about your destination, its nature or location, but open, it will become less and less familiar,

Don't then backtrack to the comfort of the known or you'll just go round in circles and never arrive.

Be careful of roads with too many warnings and instructions such as 'this is the *only* way to the centre', 'keep off the grass', 'beware of the bull', 'no left turn – no right turn', or 'trespassers will be prosecuted'.

If you followed such admonitions slavishly you would find the road had become a treadmill leading no where.

A few general directions will however help you at the beginning, a compass bearing to follow perhaps and some advice from experienced travellers about avoiding or dealing with flash floods avalanches waterless deserts sunburn rogue elephants ghosts mirages mermaids and similar hazards.

Don't fear to leave the track if the going is too easy and you feel moved to take a short cut up the crumbling mountain side or through the steaming swamp (but at the same time don't be romantic about your capabilities);

Your fellow travellers will urge you to come back, shout abuse or shake their heads sadly thinking you are lost,

But if you can avoid either anger or giving up some of them may come with you, which would be desirable because a few good companions are helpful just as the wrong ones hold you back,

But you must be prepared for loneliness.

At the right time you will converge with others who started off on quite different routes with quite different ideas about finding the centre or indeed where or what it is,

But having come this far all are united;

How happy then to travel knowing that all paths have flowed together to form a single universal highway.

Social Ecology Series: Books in Print

Ariadne's Awakening, M. Matthews, S. Schaefer & B. Staley

Dying Forests, J. Bockemühl

Hope, Evolution and Change, J. Davy

Man on the Threshold, B. C. J. Lievegoed

Rudolf Steiner, R. Lissau

Social Ecology, M. Large

Vision in Action, C. Schaefer & T. Voors

If you have difficulties ordering from a bookshop,
you can order direct from Hawthorn Press,
Bankfield House, 13 Wallbridge, Stroud, Glos. GL5 3JA, U.K.
Telephone (045 36) 77040.